JESUS, PRAYER AND THE BIBLE FOR YOUNG READERS

DONALD MIMS

authorHOUSE

AuthorHouse™
1663 Liberty Drive
Bloomington, IN 47403
www.authorhouse.com
Phone: 833-262-8899

Published by AuthorHouse 09/24/2020

ISBN: 978-1-6655-0071-5 (sc)
ISBN: 978-1-6655-0145-3 (e)

Print information available on the last page.

Any people depicted in stock imagery provided by Getty Images are models, and such images are being used for illustrative purposes only.
Certain stock imagery © Getty Images.

This book is printed on acid-free paper.

Because of the dynamic nature of the Internet, any web addresses or links contained in this book may have changed since publication and may no longer be valid. The views expressed in this work are solely those of the author and do not necessarily reflect the views of the publisher, and the publisher hereby disclaims any responsibility for them.

KJV
Scripture taken from the King James Version of the Bible.

ACKNOWLEDGEMENTS

I want to thank so many wonderful God filled individuals, family members, and friends for their undying support of me during this spiritual journey that I have been blessed to be on. The good lord has been so extremely wonderful to me and has been an ever present help and force within my life and especially when I have needed him the most. To my loving and supporting parents, Georgia and Benjamin (Mary) Mims, I truly cannot thank you enough for the love you have afforded me throughout my life. To my aunts, uncles, cousins and true friends, I wish I could name you all, but know that I love you and thank you all from the depths of my soul for your love and support. To all of my ministry friends who are devout men and women of the clergy, I can't thank you enough for your willingness to pray and pour into me. To my Foster's Grove Church family, you all have been such a blessing. To my pastor and first lady, the great Horace Wilson, Jr. and the beautiful Ms. Barbara Wilson, I love and thank the two of you as well. To the Rev. Ricky Houser, thanks for being such a force for Christ and a true coworker and friend in ministry. To my brothers, especially my identical twin, I love you guys more than you could ever imagine. To my beautiful wife, Patrena L. Mims, you have stood by me through thick and thin and have always been an inspiration and source of strength for me. I can only hope to make you proud to call me your husband. To my two beautiful daughters, Deona and Lauren, you have always inspired me to be better and to be an inspiration for the next generation. To my late grandparents, Junior Hammond, Fred and Mable Harris, I will never forget all you have done for me. Your unconditional love and support will always stay with me. To my grandmother, Ms. Annie Mae Hammonds, your beautiful and profound sayings have inspired me in ways you'd never imagine. Please know that I love you and am always praying for you. And last, to all of my Foster Grove Baptist Church youth group members and to the many youth and teens I have had the pleasure to mentor, love and build meaningful relationships with from within the many communities, schools, group and foster homes over the past 20 or more years, thank you all as well.

Donald "Don" Mims, M. Ed, Ed. S

WHO IS JESUS?

Series 1

Jesus is God's son. Sin came into the world when Adam and Eve disobeyed God; God asked Jesus to come to make things right again. Jesus was born about 2,000 years ago, and he lived in a part of the world called the Holy Land. When he was about thirty years old, he began to preach and to heal. Three or four years later he was nailed to a cross to die. When the people who loved him went to his grave three days later, Jesus' body wasn't there. He had come back to life, just as he said he would. This is known as the resurrection.

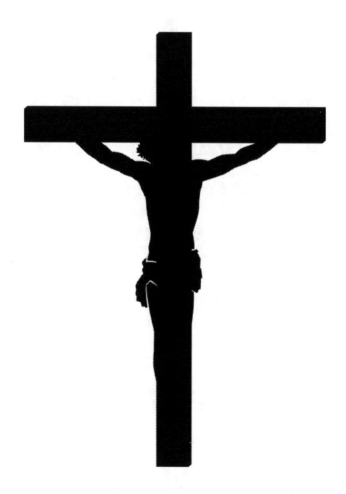

Jesus is in heaven with his father. He has not left us alone here on earth. He sent the Holy Spirit to live with us, to make us strong when we feel like giving up, to help us to care about other people when we sometimes don't feel like it, and to tell us that Jesus will always love us.

Jesus had to die. It was all part of God's plan to make right what had become so wrong because of sin. God loves us so much he sent Jesus to take our punishment. Because of Jesus, we can know for sure that God welcomes us into his loving arms, right now and when we die and go to heaven to be with him.

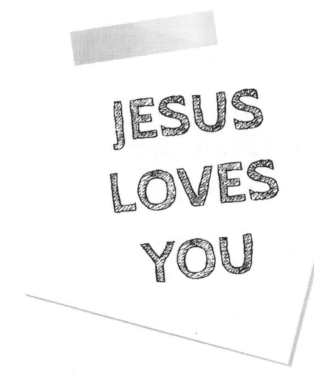

Jesus loves you more than you can ever imagine. He loves you when you moan, cry and when you laugh, when you argue with your brother or sister, and when you've had a bad day. He loves you so much that he died for you, but he isn't still dead. He is alive, and he is loving and watching over you every day.

Jesus will never stop loving you. There will be times when you wonder if Jesus is really real. There will be times when you wonder if he loves you. There will be times when you do things you shouldn't, when you act mean towards others, or lie to your parents. When you pray and tell Jesus that you have times when you doubt, when you pray and tell Jesus that you know you've done wrong and you want to do better, you can be sure that he will never let you down. He will love you your whole life long, and you will live with him forever.

You know you are a Christian when you love Jesus with all the love you can give, when you know deep down that Jesus loves you, when you believe he died to forgive your sins, when you want to live for Jesus; those are good signs that help you know you are a Christian. Sure, you're going to fail sometimes, but you will always be covered during those times of failure. He can see deep into your heart. He knows your desire to live for him, and he absolutely loves you.

WHAT IS PRAYER?

Series 2

Talking to God and or developing a habit of talking to God may seem hard to do. I suggest that youth consider starting by selecting a special time each day to pray and talk with God. I also suggest that youth consider thinking about what you'd like to say in advance of praying like, "Thank You", "I'm sorry", and or "Please help me". And then tell the Lord what's on your heart. You don't have to use fancy words. You can talk to the Lord as if he was your mother, father, friend or neighbor.

There isn't a thing you could say to him that would make him stop loving you. You can tell him when you are sad or feeling lonely. You can thank him when everything is going well, and you can depend on him when you are having a bad day. You can talk to him just in the same way you'd talk to a friend. Be mindful that a friend may let you down, your mom or dad may not always understand, but God will always listen and he'll understand.

The good lord has promised in the bible that he'll always listen to you. Psalm 66:17-19 confirms this. Also, John 16:23 confirms God's promises to listen when you pray in Jesus' name. Most importantly, the Holy Spirit lives in your heart. It helps you to know that the lord listens when you talk to him.

There is no particular way you have to pray. Closing your eyes demonstrates that you don't want anything to distract you from talking and praying to God. It's not the only way to pray. You can pray while on your knees or standing up. You can pray while watching your favorite movie or while visiting with your grandparents. You can talk with God anytime, because he is always right there with you. And, he wants you to be his friend.

WHAT IS THE BIBLE?

Series 3

The bible is a book that tells us about God. It shows us what he is like, what he has done, and what he wants us to do. It tells us about ourselves; it tells us how God made us and about how sin came into the world. It tells us about Jesus, who came to show us how much God loves us and wants to forgive our sins.

The bible was written by humans who were selected by God to write down what he wanted to say and wanted us to know. We can trust God that he worked in the writers so that they wrote down what is genuinely God's word, even though God let each writer use his own personality and style. In essence, God wrote the bible.

The people that wrote the bible lived a long time ago. Some, like Moses, lived as long ago as 3,500 years. Others, like John, lived about 1,900 years ago. In lots of ways they were people just like we are...people who had doubts, people who did some bad things and some good things as well. God used them to write down words that tell us about him and his love for us.

The bible is one of the most important ways that God uses to talk and to let you know that he is real. The bible is more than just a bunch of old stories about some people who lived a long time ago. It is God's love letter to you, assuring you that he is interested in you and will take care of you every day.

I hope you have learned something about Jesus, Prayer, and the Bible. Below are some fun facts about the Bible.

* Jesus is God's son. His parents were the Virgin Mary and Joseph.
* Jesus was born in Bethlehem. He died in Calvary.
* There are 66 books in the Bible.
* Although the Bible isn't basic at all, BIBLE means, Basic Instructions before Leaving Earth.
* The bible was written by 40 different authors.
* There are 365 fear not verses in the Bible. One for each day of the year.
* The first book of the Bible is Genesis.
* The last book of the Bible is Revelation.

* The Bible consist of two parts. The Old Testament and the New Testament.
* The Old Testament was originally written in Hebrew and has 39 books.
* The New Testament was originally written in Greek and has 27 books.
* There is a total of 185 songs in the Bible.
* The Bible was written in 3 continents. They are Asia, Africa, and Europe.
* The very last word in the Bible is Amen in the book of Revelation. Amen means "So be it".
* Prayer is simply communicating with God.

Printed in the United States
By Bookmasters